THE ORIGINAL RULES OF GOLF

FOREWORD BY TONY JACKLIN

INTRODUCTION BY DALE CONCANNON

Bodleian Library
UNIVERSITY OF OXFORD

The Bodleian Library would like to thank Archie Baird, Peter Crabtree, Olive Geddes, and Vicky Cuming for their generous help in preparing this publication.

First published in 2009 by the Bodleian Library
Broad Street, Oxford OX1 3BG

www.bodleianbookshop.co.uk

ISBN: 978 1 85124 342 6

Cover design by Dot Little
Internal series design by JCS Publishing Services Ltd
www.jcs-publishing.co.uk
Printed in England by Cromwell Press, Trowbridge, Wilts

A CIP record of this publication is available from the British Library

CONTENTS

Foreword 5

Introduction 7
   The Origins of Golf...13
   Changing Times..21
   The Silver Club and the
      First Rules.....................................26
   Then & Now 31
   What Happened Next? 35
   St Andrews Joins the Fray 39
   Back to the Future...43

The Original Rules of Golf
   Gentleman Golfers of Edinburgh, 1744 51
   The Burgess Club, 1773 55

By the la' Harry
Thus shall not go for Nothing

4

FOREWORD

I T IS NO EXAGGERATION to say that the rules of golf are the game of golf. While in other sports, a player might expect the referee to blow a whistle and arbitrate on a point of dispute, golf depends to a large degree upon self-enforcement of the rules by the participants.

Courtesy, fairness, and integrity are expected of each player. This is possible only if everyone involved understands the basic rules of golf. The rules therefore embody the spirit of the game to a degree that is almost unique in sport.

At the professional level, the highest standards of sportsmanship and personal conduct are expected. For the amateur and even casual player, golf etiquette is no less a part of the game. It is the rules of golf which allow players of all levels of skill to participate in the game on a fair and equitable level. Studying the rules and their origins is therefore an excellent way of ensuring that we all live up to the standards of etiquette expected on the course.

While the rules have evolved over the past three centuries, the original rules formed by the Gentlemen Golfers of Edinburgh all those years ago are still at the heart of golf today and continue to exert a powerful influence on the way the game is played.

Tony Jacklin

INTRODUCTION

HORACE GUTHRIE HUTCHINSON enrolled at Corpus Christi College in 1878. A talented sportsman, he won the University Cue at billiards, earned football and cricket honours, and helped make his university practically unbeatable at golf. During his time at Oxford the future (British) Amateur Golf Champion famously introduced his logic tutor William Little to the game but the author of the *Shorter Oxford English Dictionary* proved an unwilling pupil. Asked his opinion by Hutchinson, he pondered for a moment. 'Golf', he replied, 'involved little more than putting little balls into little holes with instruments singularly ill-adapted to the purpose.'

Oft repeated, his description sums up golf perfectly and for a large part of its history that is exactly how the game was played. For well over 400 years, right up until the introduction of a formalized version of the sport in the mid-eighteenth century, golf was a crude, rambunctious pastime with none of the precision of modern times. From those dark beginnings on the east coast of Scotland, rules were considered unimportant in a game whose only imperative was to get your ball into the hole in fewer blows than your opponent. If that meant blocking or stymieing your adversary's ball then so be it. If a collision sent their ball careering off-course, then all-the-better.

Yet rules dominate the modern game. At the last count there are over sixty defined terms around which the rules of play are written, with countless

more amendments, definitions, applications, and explanations. The current rule book weighs in at around 160 pages and is updated regularly by the two governing bodies of the world game, the Royal and Ancient Golf Club of St Andrews and the United States Golf Association. Contradictory to noted author Henry Longhurst's long-held belief that the rules of golf should take up no more space than that found on the back of a postcard, simplicity is no longer the name of the game.

From how to drop the ball correctly under penalty to advice on whether a hippopotamus footprint constitutes a hazard or not, there is a rule covering nearly every eventuality. Yet golf is a unique sport in the way it is policed. In everyday golf, unlike soccer, rugby, tennis and so on, there are no referees, umpire, or line judges to keep the players honest. In serious and top golf competitions, however, there are referees, with players, including professionals, marking each other's scorecards.

It is the same in the amateur game. It is an unwritten law in golf that everyone conducts themselves in a fundamentally fair and even-handed manner. With so many rules to learn,

the typical Sunday-morning enthusiast cannot be expected to know everything. Yet many carry the rule book in their bag. This is a game where cheats are quickly found out and flagrant benders of the rules find themselves under withering scrutiny from their playing partners.

For millions throughout the golfing world, the rules are not mere suggestions but the very bedrock of the game. Players are the guardians of the sport and it really does not matter if your name is Tiger Woods or Walbert P. James III—reputation is all. For centuries, fairness and good etiquette were part of the game as golfers wagered huge sums on the outcome of a match. The original thirteen rules were born out of the necessity to have a code of play when the Edinburgh Town Council presented

a Silver Club in 1744 for competition. The rules of golf were formulated by the Gentlemen Golfers of Edinburgh and penned by a Jacobite surgeon; the story of their genesis would rival many a good thriller, stretching back over five centuries on the windswept east coast of Scotland.

THE ORIGINS OF GOLF

Searching for the origins of golf has been a favourite occupation of historians since Victorian times. Any 'stick-and-ball' game bore even a fleeting similarity has been examined for evidence of an early link, with France, Holland, England, and even China all offering a possible starting point for the Royal and Ancient Game. In Roman times, a sport called *paganica* was popular with the common soldiery. Played with a *baculus incurvatus* or curved club, it involved hitting a leather-covered ball stuffed with small feathers towards a target, such as a tree stump, well or doorway. Played over open countryside, it was thought to have been introduced into Britain during the Roman occupation of the first century. Long considered a possible forerunner of golf, there is no evidence

that it survived the departure of the Romans in the third century but the ball is remarkably similar to the 'feathery' used in the early years of Scottish golf.

Since medieval times there have been many stick-and-ball games recorded as having been played in Europe. The game that we now know as golf was just one of these pastimes and its birthplace was undoubtedly the linkslands of the Scottish coast as early as the fifteenth century and possibly before. Some of its features may well have been borrowed from the French *jeu de mail* or the Dutch *kolve* or *kolf* and perhaps other games, but golf is certainly Scottish in origin.

Scotland, of course, has long been considered the 'Home of Golf'. Certainly the topography of Scotland played a pivotal role in the development and popularization of golf. Since ancient times, the sandy wasteland areas known as links proved little suited for anything other than grazing sheep, holding fairs, and playing sport. A prominent feature of many Scottish east coast towns such as Aberdeen, Montrose, St Andrews, Musselburgh, and North Berwick were their links, and whilst the definitive origins of the game are unknown these were certainly the cradle in which golf was nurtured.

The first written reference to golf came on 6 March 1457. With England threatening invasion from the south, King James II, at his Parliament in Edinburgh, banned both football and golf throughout Scotland. He was concerned that his subjects were spending too much time on these sports and not enough practising archery. He ordained and decreed 'that ye fut bawe and ye golf be utterly cryt done and not usyt' and that a pair of targets be made at all parish kirks and shooting be practised each Sunday.

Revealing how popular and widespread golf must have been in the fifteenth century, golf, gouf, goff or gowfe as it was alternatively known, not only survived, but thrived. Even the all-powerful Scottish Church found the game troublesome. In 1610, the Session Records of South Leith Parish Church ordered that anyone caught playing golf on the Sabbath would be fined twenty shillings, with guilty parties forced to repent from the pulpit the

following Sunday. Draconian as these fines were, it was known that some clergymen were secret golfers themselves. The Bishop of Galloway, for example, dreamed that two men attacked him while he was out playing on Leith Links in 1619. Many blamed an attack of conscience because he had been seen playing golf during Lent. Racked with guilt, he

reportedly threw down his clubs, took to his bed, and died soon after!

Widening its appeal, golf gradually became more acceptable to Church and State. After the Union of the Crowns in 1603, Scotland saw an extended period of peace, with the game transported south to London by James VI, who acceded to the English throne (as James I of England) after the death of Elizabeth I. Introduced to the game by his mother, Mary, Queen of Scots, he appointed William Mayne of Edinburgh as royal club-maker for life. Then, after restricting the amount of feather golf balls imported into Scotland from Holland, he granted an exclusive twenty-one-year monopoly to Quartermaster James Melville in 1618. He passed his love of golf to his son, King Charles I, who was on Leith Links when news of the Irish Rebellion was brought to him in 1642.

Leith Links would also play a vital role in the evolution of the game. By the demise of the Stuart line in 1714, it had been used for golf for over 300 years. With holes measuring 414, 461, 426,

495, and 435 yards respectively, the testing five-hole layout was situated on common land within a short distance of Edinburgh's most important port. Being close to a busy thoroughfare, these links must have been a noisy, bustling place to play golf in the early eighteenth century as the general populace mingled with the wealthy merchant with his handmade clubs and feathery balls.

Yet throughout the long period that golf had been played in Scotland, no defined set rules were in existence—or at least none we know about. The game obviously had some rules but they were on an ad hoc basis and were tailored to suit the course, the town, the village, and the people who played it. Golf was no longer the primitive game

that it had been and social attitudes were changing along with the times. By the mid-1700s, Scottish golf would become more organized as the desire for social exclusivity grew. From costermongers to bakers, lawyers to accountants, private clubs and societies were being established along class lines and, although the links were situated on public land, there was no reason why the upper and lower classes should mix. It seemed the day of the first organized golf club was coming.

CHANGING TIMES

By 1740, strong trading links with Holland and France had brought a period of relative prosperity to Scotland. Many Edinburgh merchants had earned fortunes trading in wool and cotton and enjoyed the privileges and respect their wealth had brought. With golf a favoured pastime, it was natural to want this privilege and respect extended to the links. Banding together with others of the same class and social standing, they began to segregate themselves into small golfing groups. Having the time and money to spend on their leisure activities, these so-called 'Gentlemen Golfers' were able to indulge in the habit of arranging matches during weekdays—something that the humble artisans could never afford to do. They also indulged in much wining and dining after their matches. The conviviality of such occasions was fuelled by fines of claret, porter, and spirits for such misdemeanours as not wearing the society uniform upon the links. Those early golfers who could afford it certainly saw no merit in self-denial.

Another factor in the widening social gap was the growing use of caddies. A typical set of clubs at this time numbered approximately five long-nose woods and one iron. Local people, who carried them underarm, were employed to perform this task and it became a useful way to supplement a fairly meagre existence. Naturally the poorer classes could never afford caddies themselves or even the expensive clubs and feather balls they carried around. For the first time in its history, Scottish golf now had two distinct and wholly separate golfing classes and while the links remained open to all, these Gentlemen Golfers increasingly acquired a distinct status.

These well-to-do golfers increasingly played the game adorned in brightly coloured coats, and society uniforms came into being. Naturally, most played in hunting pink (red) but green, blue, and even grey jackets would come into use. An important element in the growing segregation, clothing eventually grew to include golfing breeches and nailed shoes

By the second quarter of the eighteenth century 'Match Days' had become a regular occurrence at Edinburgh's two most popular links—Leith in the east and Bruntsfield in the centre of the city near the Castle. Banding together in small groups, Leith Links became home to one of the earliest and most influential of these original societies—the Gentleman Golfers of Edinburgh.

Like others, the fledgling Thistle Club would compete at golf before retiring to a nearby tavern

known as Luckie Clephan's. With a strong Masonic influence underlying the whole occasion, post-match feasts became a popular feature of such gatherings. A time for ritualized speech making, holding inquests into the day's play, making and settling wagers, it was above all an opportunity to consume copious amounts of wine and port. In his 1771 novel *The Expedition of Humphrey Clinker* Tobias Smollett offers a flavour of the rich social mix that still pervaded the links:

> Hard by, in the fields called the Links, the citizens of Edinburgh divert themselves at a game called Golf. Of this diversion the Scots are so fond, that, when the weather will permit, you may see a multitude of all ranks, from the senator of justice to the lowest tradesman, mingled together, in their shirts, and following the balls with the utmost eagerness.

Gambling was an obvious attraction during this period, with golf offering plenty of opportunities to wager large sums not only on your own match, but on others as well. In 1724, 'a solemn match at golf' took place on Leith Links between the Honourable Alexander Elphinstone and Captain of the Edinburgh City Guard, John Porteous. With the players competing for the huge sum of twenty guineas, it was important enough to be reported in a local newspaper: 'The reputation of the players for skill excited great interest,' the early golf journalist wrote, 'and the match was attended by James, Duke of Hamilton, George, Earl of Morton and a vast crowd of spectators.'

On this occasion, Elphinstone was the winner but this type of big money wager was not uncommon. Whether it was cards, horseracing, or betting on the outcome of a prize fight, gambling was considered a suitable pastime for the upper classes. Golf now came into that category and while twenty guineas was a huge amount of money to bet on such a match, it probably paled into insignificance compared to the amount bet outside the ropes by onlookers!

With large raucous crowds following this and other big money matches that followed, golf's popularity among the well-to-do members of Edinburgh society grew ever stronger. The only thing the game needed now was a competition in which a large group of golfers could compete. To achieve that, you needed a suitable venue, an attractive prize, and a set of rules acceptable to all. By spring 1744, all those elements would be in place.

THE SILVER CLUB AND THE
FIRST RULES

The first official set of rules was introduced in March 1744. But it would be a mistake to assume that golf was not played under strict guidelines before that date. As contemporary newspaper reports show, large sums were often wagered on individual matches and it is correct to assume they must have been conducted under widely acceptable guidelines; guidelines under which friends could play even if there was little or nothing on the outcome.

So why did these Gentlemen Golfers suddenly feel the need to write them down? With 'holes won' (match play) the preferred method of play at Leith Links, individual matches were keenly contested but there was a growing desire for a competition in which all could take part. Proposing to organize one, 'Several Gentlemen of Honour, Skilfull in the Ancient and Healthful Exercise of the Golf,' petitioned Edinburgh City Council in March 1744 to provide them with a Silver Club to be played for annually on the Links of Leith. The response was positive, with the competition being open to 'Noblemen or Gentlemen, or other golfers, from any part of Great Britain or Ireland'. 'The town council asked the Gentlemen Golfers to draw up 'Such Articles and Conditions, as to them Seem'd most Expedient, as proper Regulations…'. This was duly done—they were detailed, specific,—and the first rules of golf came into being.

The town council, having drawn up an 'Act of Council' on 7 March 1744 for the regulations for the competition of the Silver Club, effectively incorporated the 'Company of Gentleman Golfers'. The first minute book opens with a transcript of the Act, and the date set for the competion, 2 April 1744—is regarded as the date of formation of what was later to become the 'Honourable Company of Edinburgh Golfers'.

Having given a silver arrow to the Royal Company of (Edinburgh) Archers back in 1709, the town council agreed for a full-size silver club to be supplied on the condition that it did not cost in excess of fifteen pounds sterling (in the event it cost £17 4s 3d). To cover the prize money, an entry fee of five shillings was levied from each competitor, with the total fund going to the winner. The victor would be declared Captain of the Golf for the forthcoming year, with the power to officiate on any dispute that might arise in future competitions. Plus he would be required to fix a silver replica of a ball to commemorate his victory (a tradition that continues to this day).

Members of the fledgling Gentleman Golfers of Edinburgh were invited to enter the competition scheduled for 2 April 1744, along with other prominent golfers from the local area. But what rules would they play under? Those who played regularly at Leith knew what hazards to expect and could act accordingly, but what about those competitors who played the majority of their golf at Bruntsfield,

Musselburgh, or even far away St Andrews? And how do you find one winner when each entrant had cut their competitive teeth on individual match play?

The solution they chose has caused much debate among golfing historians over the years. According to a contemporary account in the *Scots Magazine*, competitors would be sent out in pairs or, 'by three's if their number be great, by lot; that the player who shall have won the greater number of holes be victor, and if two or more shall be an equal number, that they play a round by themselves in order to determine the match'.

While stroke play was in fairly common use by the Gentleman Golfers not long after, the winner on this occasion was not the player with the lowest score but the one with most holes 'won'. (For example, if one player scored 3 at the first hole and ten competitors scored 4 he would be 'ten-holes to the good' or 'up'. This would then apply for each hole played.) Equally, it is also possible that the ten entrants played five individual matches on the day with the winner being the most 'holes up' on his opponents. Sadly, the records of the present-day Honourable Company do not confirm it either way and it shall remain for now a subject for further research.

What we do know is that to facilitate the smooth running of the event the Gentleman Golfers provided a list of thirteen rules by which all competitors would abide. Penned by local surgeon, John Rattray, these rules would prove groundbreaking in golfing terms. Establishing guidelines by which the world would play the game for the next 250 years, they detailed what action should be taken in any given situation. Forever known as the 'Leith Code' it covered, among other things, outside interference, order of play, teeing-off, and was the first to define the stroke and distance penalty for the loss of a ball in a hazard. Today, the competition for the Silver Club is widely accepted as the first official golf tournament ever held.

THEN & NOW:
ORIGINAL AND CONTEMPORARY RULES COMPARED

While modern golfers will recognize many of the thirteen rules (see pp. 51-52), a brief explanation might prove helpful. For example, Rule 1 discusses teeing-up, 'within a club's length of the hole'. Common practice at the time, a handful of sand was removed from the hole and a raised platform built to accommodate the next tee shot. (With the invention of the golf tee well over a century away, the effect on short putts must have been quite profound.) Later extended to two club lengths, the rule remained in general use until the 1870s, when separate teeing grounds were introduced.

Rule 2: This deals with the fundamental belief that golf is a static ball game. While there is no recorded incident of a golf ball being struck 'shinty-style' it is interesting to find the term 'on the ground' noted so prominently. Equally, it has been suggested that this rule stopped any player building a platform to raise his ball to a much higher level, but quite what advantage this would proffer is unsure.

Rule 3: The Leith Code's insistence that no golfer should change his ball before striking off is interesting in both historic and economic terms. Expensive to purchase, leather-covered feathery golf balls were prone to falling apart in wet weather and without this observance, the rich player with a large reserve might hold an unfair advantage over someone less well off.

Rule 4: The 'loose element' rule still applies today on both the putting green and in bunkers. The only minor difference is that it was only applied within a club's length of the hole on the 'fair green' and rarely do modern-day players face removing 'bones' from the sand.

Rule 5: Dropping under penalty behind a hazard is something that every modern golfer will recognize. The difference is that back in 1744 the player was allowed to tee-up his ball after taking the penalty.

Rule 6: A similar rule applies today. The only difference is that no mention is made of not cleaning the ball once it has been lifted.

Rule 7: The idea that you do not interfere with your opponent's ball on the green is fundamental to golf. No doubt this harks back to the dark ages of the game when a player could use his ball to strike another by deliberately aiming away from the hole.

Rule 8: This is the stroke-and-distance rule that still applies today.

Rule 9: Once again, the idea that you cannot mark your way to the hole on the putting green is fundamental to the modern game.

Rule 10: The 'outside agencies' rule still applies today but instead of horses and dogs we have ball-washers, bunker rakes, and electric golf buggies. That said, distractions like those mentioned were fairly typical as the (golf) links themselves were on common land.

Rule 11: Modern equipment is far more resilient that the ancient long-nose club of the mid-nineteenth century and is not prone to breaking at the top of the backswing, making such incidents extremely rare. That said, the penalty would be exactly the same if the downswing had been completed.

Rule 12: The idea that 'he whose ball lies farthest from the hole is obliged to play first' has been an accepted tenet of golf for centuries. The only time it does not apply is in a fourball match play situation when one partner can request another to play out of turn to gain some advantage.

Rule 13: This is the only one dealing specifically with the 'hazards' found on Leith Links. Essentially a 'local' rule, it details various elements of the terrain and offers advice on how they should be overcome. (The links had seen action as both a battleground and a headquarters for Cromwellian forces during the English Civil War, with grassy mounds at the eastern end marking former cannon emplacements.)

WHAT HAPPENED NEXT?

The competition went ahead with eleven players, who were named as Robert Biggar, James Carmichael, Richard Cockburn, William Crosse, David and Hew Dalrymple, James Gordon, the Honourable James Leslie, George Suttie, James Veith, and John Rattray, (Reflecting the high social class of those who competed, Duncan Forbes, President of the Court of Session, apparently put his name down for the competition, but did not play.)

Played over the five-hole Leith Links on 2 April 1744, it was fitting that the first winner of the Silver Club was the undoubted driving force behind the

inaugural competition, John Rattray. A founder member of the Gentleman Golfers of Edinburgh (later established as the Honourable Company of Edinburgh Golfers) and signatory to the original set of rules, he was a hugely respected figure in Edinburgh society. Widely credited with drawing up the 'Leith Code', he was praised for his sporting prowess in Thomas Mathison's heroi-comical poem 'The Goff', published in 1743.

A talented golfer, Rattray successfully defended his title the following year. Sadly, it would not be the case in 1746; he was unable to make a third successive attempt at the title, having been arrested as a Jacobite rebel after Bonnie Prince Charlie's disastrous defeat at Culloden. Re-arrested in Edinburgh in May, he was sent to London under house arrest before he was finally released in 1747 as part of a general amnesty. Returning to his life as a surgeon, Rattray won for the third and final time in 1751.

Certainly the world of golf owes John Rattray and his fellow devotees a debt of gratitude for establishing what would eventually become the first universally acceptable set of rules. Until that point, golf was a parochial sport played on an ad hoc basis with rules tailored to the particular course and conditions. What the players did not realize at the time was how vital such a set of guidelines would be to the development of the game in Scotland. Golf needed the 'Leith Code' just as an amateur player needs a good putting stroke. And while many of the rules published in March 1744 were probably in use throughout the Edinburgh area and elsewhere some years before, the clarity and vision displayed by these Gentlemen Golfers is almost breathtaking.

St Andrews Joins the Fray

Exactly a decade after the Gentleman Golfers of Edinburgh had played for the Silver Club, twenty-two 'Noblemen and Gentlemen of Fife… being Admirers of the Ancient and healthfull Exercise of the Golf, and at the same time having the Interest and prosperity of the Ancient City of St Andrews at heart, being the Alma Mater of the Golf, Did in the year of our Lord 1754 Contribute for a Silver Club having a St Andrew Engraved on the head thereof, to be played for on the Links of St Andrews upon the 14th day of May said year and yearly in time coming…', thus forming the Society of St Andrews Golfers.

Taking a lead from the Gentleman Golfers of Edinburgh, they raised enough funds to purchase their own silver club as a competition prize. Like the competition at Leith, the St Andrews event was open to all and played under the original Leith Code. Indeed, the St Andrews players accepted the thirteen rules almost word for word, including (somewhat strangely) Rule 13, which described how to negotiate the 'Scholar's Holes', and 'Soldier's Lines' found at Leith Links!

The first winner was local merchant William Landale, who was immediately installed as the first Captain of a society that would eventually evolve into the Royal and Ancient Golf Club of St Andrews. Confirming the elite nature of these early golfing societies, St Andrews would restrict future competitions to members only, no doubt to avoid the possibility of an 'outsider' or 'undesirable' winning the Silver Club and thus becoming 'Captain of the Golf'. In 1764 the Gentleman Golfers of Edinburgh made application to Edinburgh City Council, requesting that the Silver Club competition be restricted to 'Such Noblemen and Gentlemen as they approve to be Members of the Company of Golfers'.

Elsewhere each club either adopted the 1744 rules or formulated ones of their own to suit their course. The Burgess Club, for example, had been in existence since 1735 but lagged behind the Gentleman Golfers of Edinburgh and Society of St Andrews Golfers in actually recording a set of rules. Taking its membership from a far wider cross-section of Scottish society, the majority were lawyers with the remainder comprising bakers, rope-makers, window-makers, stonemasons and even a hairdresser!

Originally based at Bruntsfield, now on the western edge of Edinburgh, this particular society centred its social activities round a rather raucous hostelry situated hard by the links, named The Golf Tavern. Still there today, it was owned by Thomas Combs, who made a private room available on match days and converted a storeroom into a locker room for the members, (something the Gentleman Golfers at Leith could only dream of). Like many similar groups, the Burgess Club had their own set of rules and published these in 1773. This is the third oldest set of rules in existence, and it is interesting to compare it with the original Leith Code from which it drew its inspiration (see pp 55–58).

BACK TO THE FUTURE

As the popularity of the game grew over the next
two decades it was inevitable that even more
detailed sets of rules would be implemented.
Both the Society of St Andrews Golfers and the
Gentleman Golfers of Edinburgh (later to become
the Honourable Company of Edinburgh Golfers)
amended the original Leith Code at various times,
including a 1758 addition to the original Articles &
Laws of the Leith Code that read:

> The 5th, and 13th Articles of the foregoing
> Laws having occasioned frequent Disputes
> It is found Convenient That in all time
> Coming, the Law Shall be, That in no Case
> Whatever a Ball Shall be Lifted without
> losing a Stroke Except it is in the Scholars
> holes When it may be taken out teed and
> played with any Iron Club without losing a
> Stroke—And in all other Cases the Ball must
> be Played where it lyes Except it is at least
> half Covered with Water or filth When it
> may, if the Player Chuses be taken out Teed
> and Played with any Club upon Loosing a
> Stroke.

Establishing a pattern that has extended to modern times where the rules are revised every four years, the Leith Code was amended again in 1775. The original thirteen rules formed the basis for the new guidelines that followed from Bruntsfield in 1776, Aberdeen Golf Club in 1783 and Crail in 1786. In 1824, the Secretary of Aberdeen wrote to the (Edinburgh) Thistle Golf Club thanking them for a copy of Rules of the Thistle Golf Club sent by member John Cundell. The first reviewer of golf's earliest guidelines, he commented: 'I have little doubt that these historical recollections will have a permanency with the Game itself.'

He was probably right. As the game's popularity spread throughout the world, it was inevitable that allowances would be made within the rules for

terrain and conditions so different to those found in Scotland. Improvements in equipment also meant that rules had to be constantly updated and this is still the case today.

The game expanded greatly in the second half of the nineteenth century because of the introduction of the cheaper and more durable *gutta percha* ball which replaced the feathery around 1850. With the introduction of national match play and stroke play tournaments, it became imperative that there be a universal set of rules observed by all. In 1897, the Royal and Ancient Golf Club (the R&A) was asked by other leading clubs to formulate such rules and the Rules of Golf Committee of the club was formed. This club thus became, together with the United States Golf Association, the governing body of the game.

Some may ask why it is, given that the Honourable Company of Edinburgh Golfers gave the game the first written rules, that the R&A became the governing body and St Andrews the 'Home of Golf'? It is a legitimate question. The answer is surely that the St Andrews course, originally twenty-two holes but reduced to eighteen in the 1760s, was far superior to all others, and certainly to the five-hole Leith course and its successor, nine-hole Musselburgh, both former homes of the Gentleman Golfers. In addition, St Andrews was a pillar of stability compared with the Gentleman Golfers, who felt obliged to up sticks and move twice before settling at Muirfield in the 1890s.

As recently as 1947, the United States Golf Association reduced the Rules of Golf from sixty-one to twenty-one in an attempt to simplify the game. So, does having more rules make the game easier? Many argue that it does. Others, like Henry Longhurst, probably considered the original thirteen rules as over-complicating matters! Whatever the answer, the game of golf looks set to endure, and for that alone we can thank John Rattray and his intrepid band of Gentleman Golfers.

Articles & Laws in Playing at Golf

1. You must Tee your Ball, within a Clubs length of the Hole.

2. Your Tee must be upon the Ground.

3. You are not to change the Ball which you Strike off the Tee.

4. You are not to remove, Stones, Bones or any Break Club, for the sake of playing your Ball, Except upon the fair Green & that only within a Clubs length of your Ball.

5. If your Ball come among Watter, or any wattery filth, you are at liberty to take out your Ball & bringing it behind the hazard and Teeing it, you may play it with any Club and allow your Adversary a Stroke, for getting out your Ball.

6. If your Balls be found any where touching one another, You are to lift the first Ball, till you play the last.

7. At Holing, you are to play your Ball honestly for the Hole; and not to play upon your Adversary's Ball, not lying in your way to the Hole.

8. If you should lose your Ball, by its being taken up, or any other way you are to go back to the Spot, where you struck last, & drop another Ball, And allow your adversary a Stroke for the misfortune.

9. No man at Holing his Ball, is to be allowed, to mark his way to the Hole with his Club, or any thing else.

10. If a Ball be stopp'd by any person, Horse, Dog, or any thing else, The Ball so stop'd must be play'd, where it lies.

11. If you draw your Club in order to Strike & proceed so far in the Stroke, as to be bringing down your Club; If then, your Club shall break, any way, it is to be Accounted a Stroke.

ARTICLES & LAWS IN PLAYING AT GOLF

[GENTLEMAN GOLFERS OF EDINBURGH, 1744]

1. You must Tee your Ball, within a Club's length of the Hole.
2. Your Tee must be upon the Ground.
3. You are not to change the Ball which you Strike off the Tee.
4. You are not to remove, Stones, Bones or any Break Club for the sake of playing your Ball, Except upon the fair Green, & that only within a Club's length of your Ball.
5. If your Ball come among Water, or any wattery filth, you are at liberty to take out your Ball & bringing it behind the hazard and Teeing it, you may play it with any Club and allow your Adversary a Stroke for so getting out your Ball.
6. If your Balls be found any where touching one another, you are to lift the first Ball till you play the last.
7. At Holling, you are to play your Ball honestly for the Hole, and, not to play on your Adversary's Ball, not lying in your way to the Hole.

8. If you should lose your Ball, by it's being taken up, or in any other way, you are to go back to the Spot, where you struck last, & drop another Ball and allow your adversary a Stroke for the misfortune.

9. No man at Holling his Ball is allowed to mark his way to the Hole with his Club or any thing else.

10. If a Ball be stopp'd by any person, Horse, Dog, or any thing else, the Ball so stop'd must be played, where it lyes.

11. If you draw your Club in order to Strike & proceed so far in the Stroke, as to be bringing down your Club; If then your Club shall break, in any way, it is to be accounted as a Stroke.

12. He whose Ball lyes farthest from the Hole is obliged to play first.

13. Neither Trench, Ditch or Dyke, made for the preservation of the Links, nor the Scholar's Holes, or the Soldiers Lines, Shall be accounted a Hazard; But the Ball is to be taken out, Teed, and played with any Iron Club.

John Rattray, Cp^{tn}